BORED NO MORE!

The ABCs of What to Do When There's Nothing to Do

by **Julie Reiters**

Abrams Appleseed
New York

Act out a play

Bounce a ball

Dance down the hall

Explore the basement

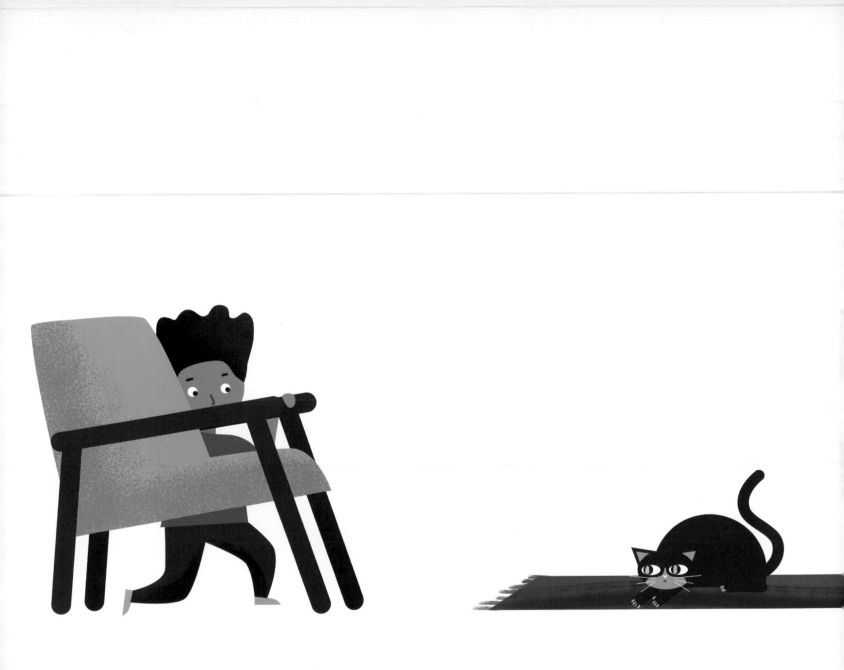

Face your fear

Grow a plant

Invent something

Jump on the bed

Knit a hat

Or **Lounge** instead

Make lots of art

Nestle down with a book

Observe a tree

Plan a meal to cook

Question things

Rock and roll

My Grandma
5 Nice Little Street
Cute Town, USA

Send a note

Unclutter your closet

Volunteer in some way

Write a poem

X out each day

Yes, yawn!
It can get boring at home.

So go **Zest** things up
with an idea from this poem!

For my parents

The artwork for this book was created digitally.

Library of Congress Control Number 2021945979
ISBN 978-1-4197-6077-8

Text and illustrations © 2022 Julie Reiters
Book design by Jade Rector

Printed and bound in China
10 9 8 7 6 5 4 3 2 1

For bulk discount inquiries, contact specialsales@abramsbooks.com.

ABRAMS The Art of Books
195 Broadway, New York, NY 10007
abramsbooks.com